Joseph Cornell:
The Man Who Loved Sparrows

Joseph Cornell:
The Man Who Loved Sparrows

Poems by

Tana Miller and Jan Zlotnik Schmidt

© 2024 Tana Miller and Jan Zlotnik Schmidt. All rights reserved.
This material may not be reproduced in any form, published,
reprinted, recorded, performed, broadcast,
rewritten, or redistributed without
the explicit permission of Tana Miller and Jan Zlotnik Schmidt.
All such actions are strictly prohibited by law.

Cover design by Shay Culligan
Cover art by Tana Miller
Author photo (Tana Miller) by Natasha Zajac
Author photo (Jan Zlotnik Schmidt) by Robin Weinstein/SUNY
New Paltz

ISBN: 978-1-63980-576-1

Kelsay Books
502 South 1040 East, A-119
American Fork, Utah 84003
Kelsaybooks.com

Acknowledgments

We thank the editors of the publications in which these poems first appeared.

Global Poemic: Jan Zlotnik Schmidt, "Houdini and Cornell: The Lure of Boxed in Worlds," later anthologized in *Rethinking the Ground Rules: Works by the Hudson Valley Women's Writing Group (Mediacs Press)*
Lightwoodpress.com (Winter Issue #16): Jan Zlotnik Schmidt, "Joseph Cornell: The Man Who Loved Sparrows," Tana Miller, "Joseph Cornell Teaches Me How to Write a Poem with No Words"

We also are thankful for the support of our families who listened to endless discussions about Joseph Cornell and his work, the Hudson Valley Women's Writing Group, and Laurence Carr, who read and provided invaluable feedback on a draft version of this chapbook.

Contents

L'Amour Eternel   11

Part I   Cornell's Theater of the Mind

Hitchhike Through Cornell's Theater of the Mind   15
Joseph Cornell Teaches Me How to Write a Poem
    with No Words   17
Joseph Cornell and Houdini: The Lure of Boxed
    in Worlds   19
Joseph Cornell Feared Infinity, Too   21

Part II   Worlds to Offer One Another

I Would Like to Show You the Infinite Splendor
    of Stardust in the Universe   25
Robert and Joseph   27
Who Are You Silly Betty and
    Where Have All Your Collages Gone?   29
Harry Houdini and Joseph Cornell: Dreaming   31

Part III   Silent Bursts of Prophecy

The White-Breasted Cockatoo and the Silenced
    Muse   35
The Great White Cockatoo: Time and Memory
    (Cockatoo with Watch Faces, Circa 1949)   37
Do Dried Wings Speak?
    (Juan Gris Series—Untitled, Circa 1958)   38
Grand Hotel Bon Port
    (Grand Hotel Bon Port, Circa 1959–1960)   39
The Last Cockatoo Box
    (Untitled Except for L'Abeille,
    Circa 1959–1960)   40

Part IV   A World Apart   41

Joseph Cornell's Bubble Box and "The Man
  Blowing Bubbles"   43
My Box Smells Like Old Cigarettes   44
The Medici Slot Machine   45
The Blue Peninsula   46
Bebe Marie   47
Through a Glass, Darkly   48
Cornell and the Sparrows   49

Biography of Joseph Cornell   51

L'Amour Eternel

Tana Miller

I'm obsessed with a dead man
not by any means the first time
I have fallen into such a sublime abyss
he was a tall thin bird-man   all beak and bones
kept himself alive for decades on stale
chocolate cake and catnaps
he's for me   he's my man
Joseph Cornell   artist   stalker of infinity
present-giver letter-writer opera-goer
filled box-after-box with eternity to be
glassed-in stacked-up sometimes sold given away
do I have a chance with him at almost eighty?
(he liked young girls   often worrisomely young)
I am tired   clumsy   unsure on my feet
(he loved ballerinas movie stars nimble waitresses
artists writers   both dead and alive)
could he love a plain amo amas amat woman?
(my sucre-man   a devoted Francophile
declared French the true language of love)
wait I have a plan:

when I die and live in paradise
I'll don lacey feathers
and pale pink toe shoes   I'll sing to him
like the ancient Sirens sang to sailors:
        Mon homme,
           Je t'apporte un ciel etoile plein
              D'amour eternel*

* My Man, I bring you a starry sky full of eternal love.

Part I

Cornell's Theater of the Mind

Hitchhike Through Cornell's Theater of the Mind

Tana Miller

Joseph   take my hand in yours
grasp it within your long slim fingers
let's fly together
high higher

two shimmering dots
entwined peepholes
out to see the universe
explore past present future

you: leave behind your musty
paper mountains, trinkets
I: my overused thesaurus
and pedantic poetry tomes

your neighbor will feed
your beloved sparrows
I will give away my dog
tell my cat to fend for herself

take me to your childhood
your mother father in their
wood paneled Nyack parlor
sisters   shiny hair adorned
with giant satin hairbows

dear dear cheerful Robert
bound tight by his own wayward
muscles will smile at us
wish us all good things

we can travel to see
Medici's golden doors
visit grand old world hotels
burned to the ground centuries ago

every patron now morphed to empty
eye sockets   gaping mouth holes   watch
your beloved Fannie Cerrito dance *Ondine*
stop to see Gris' snow white cockatoo

let us be sure to visit Miss Emily
we'll walk in her garden
tell her how much we enjoy her rhymes
and like her near-rhymes even more

we will follow your celestial maps through
intergalactic gas clouds   ride
comets' fiery tails with Bebe Marie
shrieking between us

Please don't leave me behind
tied to this tiresome earth
this failing planet
this crooked little house

let me crawl inside your magic mind
and fly with you
high higher

Joseph Cornell Teaches Me How to Write a Poem with No Words

Tana Miller

we sit in the tiny pack-rat dining room
in his family house at 3708 Utopia Parkway
Joseph Cornell   tall   craggy   pours tea
while his gruff matron-mother huffs-
puffs in the adjoining kitchen
and his brother Robert sits in his wheel chair
forever confined to the living room

let's see Cornell says and pulls out a dossier
from the haphazard multitude of boxes
stuffed in a mahogany credenza

well for me   first something catches my eye
or I think or dream something
or someone tells me about a dream
and whatever it is sticks   grows
next I collect bits: things like watches
 feathers maps old letters   any flotsam/jetsam
that like the moon endlessly reflecting the sun's light
mirrors that thing pounding within my brain

he frowns sips his tea   opens the box
his fingers sift through the broken dolls
old photographs   caress a tiny compass

then   you know   choose what is right
arrange rearrange discard cut paste trim fold
be careful   don't make it about yourself   make it about
whatever put down a taproot in your mind   he paused
for a moment then whispered   *never forget surprises*
artists must be magicians   all art requires white magic

his troll-mother announces from the kitchen doorway
Joseph your brother needs his walk now
isn't it time your friend left?

Joseph Cornell hurriedly unfolds his grasshopper length
I jump up   kiss his papery cheek
thank you I say
he doesn't reply
he doesn't walk me to the door
no one says goodbye

Joseph Cornell and Houdini: The Lure of Boxed in Worlds

Jan Zlotnik Schmidt

(Joseph Cornell watched Houdini perform at Coney Island in 1905 when he was a young boy.)

There are all kinds of boxed in worlds.
Boxes that trap memory.
Boxes that enclose and hold in desire.

A miniature woman, looking like Frieda Kahlo,
is suspended in her shallow wooden box.
Held up by threads, filaments attached
to a firmament in wood.
Perched in air, her cobalt
flowered skirt fanned out like a miniature
parasol, she hangs there paralyzed
in her etherized world.
Waiting to be set free. Or maybe not.
Maybe she's suspended in a moment of desire.

In another box the firmament is dreamed
black with specks of stars, a petrified cosmos.
Miniature constellations, like flecks of white dust,
splatters of paint in patterns, held in place.
Orion, Ursa Major, Cassiopeia, the North Star
in a spangling of hope. And in the front of the box
fluted large emptied wine glasses speak
of once human presence. A couple perhaps
staring out at the night sky. Remembering their youth.
Their desire to break free. Their unfettered longing.

Did the young boy who watched Houdini
swathed in black cloth then shut in a trunk
and finally emerge to gasping crowds
imagine the lure of boxes trunks and closed in spaces?
What they could provide.

And did Houdini love that feeling of crouching
wreathed in chains, inside a trunk,
in utter darkness set down in the sea?
Hunched over, did he have the pleasure of
suspended motion, of hearing only his sharp intakes of breath?
Did time stop for an instant as he remembered
his surge to the surface of the sea
then the quiet return to dark depths?

Did they both crave circumscribed worlds?
That solitude, that silence,
that stillness of memory?

Joseph Cornell Feared Infinity, Too

Tana Miller

I Encounter the Concept of Infinity

I was eight-years-old   stringy
runny-nosed when Mrs. Healy
my third grade teacher   announced
our earth swirled around the sun
within a limitless universe
where none of us could possibly survive
her grand finale was a worn filmstrip
entitled *The Universe is Part of our Home*
I stared at the fire-ball sun shimmering
dangerously as it straddled the earth's horizon
the lonely pocked moon imprisoned
within the boundless black skies
planets   Red giants   White dwarfs
wandering without a plan   asteroids comets
scraped back my wooden chair
hurried to the girl's bathroom
wrapped my arms around
the cool porcelain toilet
the brown tile floor
spun like whirling dervishes
the florescent lights screamed in fear
I threw up and threw up

I never told anyone
there was no one to tell

Joseph Cornell Afloat in the Universe

a huge hand reached into Cornell's world
flipped it upside down
tossed it aside

overnight: fatherless   moneyless
sent to cold starchy Phillips Academy
where he kept to himself
made no friends
made no enemies
ignored assignments
read and read and read
managed   barely   until
the astronomy class
that introduced stars moons

asteroids distant suns
and the concept of no beginning
no end   cold airless space

body raging mind raging
shaking crying day-and-night
sent home to learn to manage
he had to crawl back
spend the rest of his life
learning to manage

Part II

Worlds to Offer One Another

I Would Like to Show You the Infinite Splendor of Stardust in the Universe*

Tana Miller

of course Yayoi Kusama and Joseph Cornell were friends
she was a child-woman when they met
exactly his type   decked out in her red
polka dotted tights   a shiny gorilla fur coat

when he gazed down at her
his old patrician face crinkled with love
not that any serious hanky-panky went on
both were obsessed/repulsed by sex

they had worlds to offer one another
she: boundless shiny polka dots
painted on walls flesh chairs couches horses

he: invitations to visit Utopia Parkway
to meet famous artists his family   to see
the marbles photographs birds maps dolls
stuffed into any crevasse in the tiny house
waiting to be cut pasted arranged in boxes
sealed forever under glass sold displayed

listen love   can you hear his boxes moaning
with desire   loneliness
endlessly whispering metaphors
images to evoke our own lost childhoods
our fears our obsessions?
you and I are polka dots as well

look at the black dots Yayoi painted
on the octopus sculpture at the botanical garden
do you see my dot? your dot
is next to mine   they touch
as they whirl through infinity
forever linked

*title of an art work by Yayoi Kusama

Robert and Joseph

Tana Miller

was god watching the Cornell brothers
when they morphed into conjoined twins?
combined two strong legs three strong arms*
one despairing heart one perfect soul

Joseph   the eldest   had muscles
an artist   shy caring brilliant
obsessive   full of seething terror
Joseph named Robert the virtuous brother

Robert   younger   helpless   outgoing
unable to walk   speak beyond a grunt   feed himself
two good men welded into one
for better   for worse   for ever

as boys they played endless
games of checkers parcheesi
Joseph brought Robert bits from the world
model trains tops shiny paper

praised his rabbit drawings
took him outdoors to see cars
trains birds flowers people
fed him bathed him

later   when they were men   Joseph
brought his artist friends to meet Robert
laid them at his brother's feet
like a proud cat bringing his beloved a mouse

Joseph shaved Robert   washed his hair
heard his grunts and growls
as pure soprano tones
loved him   always loved him

wished above all things
he could stop time
fly with Robert around the world
swim through the cosmos

they lived to be old men
grizzled   gray
ate chocolate cakes   fed the birds
played the same records again and again
one monstrous non-symmetrical clumsy
person   with a wild endlessly lasting love

*Robert only had the use of one arm.

Who Are You Silly Betty and
Where Have All Your Collages Gone?

Tana Miller

after Joseph Cornell died   his weeping
sister Betty abandoned home husband
Westhampton their egg business
camped in the empty house
on Utopia Parkway   fended
off bereaved artist friends
Christian Scientists curious strangers
cleaned out the drawers
brimming with mouse nests
scrubbed the sticky refrigerator
threw away Joseph's worn shirts
packed his bits and bobs
his plastic lobsters
his balls and dolls
his notes diaries photographs
unfinished boxes abandoned boxes
into 50 shipping crates
waved them off to the Smithsonian
to be worshipped forever amen

when Betty taped a conversation
with a Smithsonian interviewer
she began in her upper class
amused-by-it-all voice:
> *when I was young   mother and daddy*
> *noticed I was artistic   sent me to classes*
> *with Eddie Hopper   a family friend*

did Joe go as well? the interviewer asked

Betty chortled:

          oh no Joe was in love with Houdini   movies
          he was not on anyone's future artist list

          I was the family artist
          I lived for those lessons

          I did not do collages
          until later   with Joseph
          I never had much time for art
          after I married   when Joe died
          I had his art his collections books
          records diaries to see to

          anyway   one day mother
          told me I would
          no longer have lessons

I asked her why

          Mr. Hopper says you are too silly
          not to waste our money

silly silly Betty*

---

*Betty (Elizabeth Vorhees Cornell) was an American painter, collagist, mostly known as world famous artist Joseph Cornell's sister. Some of her collages were given to the Smithsonian with her brother's art and possessions. A few have been auctioned since her death. None are on view.

Harry Houdini and Joseph Cornell: Dreaming

Jan Zlotnik Schmidt

What brought the young Erich Weiss to the moment when he flew on a trapeze, tiptoed across a high wire? That moment when he wanted to drift among clouds, peel himself free of his earthly body and flesh? In an early photo he is staring into the camera, hunched, almost naked, his body in shackles and chains. He knows he will free himself with secret keys. Keys that will click open handcuffs in small European towns. He knows who he is destined to be: Harry Houdini. The Handcuff King. The Master of Escapes.

And what about Joseph Cornell? He was a boy who almost drowned in dreams. In his bedroom in Nyack, in moonlight and shadow, he made finger puppets against his wall. A rabbit. A flapping mouth. He knew the power of magic—of illusion. He dreamt of flight, of escape from the muffled tragedies of his home. Voices echoing in empty rooms. The body stilled for a moment. His mind racing, cobbling together bits and pieces of past lives.

The young man, Erich Weiss, will become Houdini—shackled in a trunk, submerged in river waters, rising from the depths like a triumphant demi-god. Or like Lazarus, from a grave buried six feet deep in earth. He will emerge and show the world that death can be outwitted.

A young Joseph watched Houdini vanish an elephant on the Hippodrome stage. The creature disappeared into darkness. Cornell's world is peopled with scenes of ruin, life left behind. The cracked wine glass, a child's wooden block with a figure of a red unicorn, small round orbs and globes of the world, discarded ticket stubs, old maps of constellations in a night sky (feathery lines and dots), birds birched on empty branches.

His deaths, the demise of dreams, the fragility of memory. In one box a miniature doll with piercing eyes stares into space, surrounded by crusted snow-silvered trees. She will stay that way forever. No weeping. Just sorrow.

Part III

Silent Bursts of Prophecy

(Shadow Boxes Inspired by Juan Gris)

The White-Breasted Cockatoo and the Silenced Muse

Jan Zlotnik Schmidt

(Homage to Juan Gris 1953–1954)

Dark and light persist in the shadowed box.
The wooden planks angled secured.
A firmament without stars.

The cockatoo a flattened cutout
is not flapping his wings
or pecking his feathers.

The white bird is perched against pasted
fragments of old newspaper clippings
WW I battles and French conquests in Algiers.

He is not unfolding his tufts
or fanning out his white crest
like an upside down parasol.

No *hello. How are you?* No simple words.
Not yet a poem not yet a protest
against his circumscribed world.

And the muse watches
from afar. She too knows
the mysteries of restraint.

She knows the pain of silence
of garbled sounds of a cut tongue
and frenzied breath.

She knows the way words lodge
in the throat never to be
unearthed. Acid in her gullet.

She knows the way her body folds
into herself   into useless dreams
or silent bursts of prophecy.

The Great White Cockatoo: Time and Memory
(Cockatoo with Watch Faces, Circa 1949)

Jan Zlotnik Schmidt

Is it 7:25 am or 7:25 pm—what does it matter?
The light filtering through is dulled
his shadow self a flattened body in the bottom of the box.

The great white cockatoo is ready to flee
to flit away—his light yellow white tuft
alert to currents of wind in his shadowed world.

He sees the faces of the timepieces.
He sees the watches preserved stopped
at the moment he lost his way.

His nomadic flight among sun-drenched
palms eucalyptus groves   hills and furrows
gone   no thick green leaves shaded with damp light at twilight.

No feathered crest unfurling to call another.
No screeches and squawks echoing through
the rain forest in a single pulse of time.

Now mute—his white wings drawn in close
to his skin. His black eyes rimmed with blue stare into space.
He remembers the sheer joy of making noise.

Frozen in this eternal moment of loss
he dreams of light of wind
his soul stripped bare and grieving.

Do Dried Wings Speak?
(Juan Gris Series—Untitled, Circa 1958)

Jan Zlotnik Schmidt

Do dried wings speak
as they fall darkened
to the bottom of the cage?

Do black curved beaks pit
against teak and sandalwood
feasting on fruit seeds and crickets?

Do they preen their lemon yellow plumage
almost ivory in night light singed by the
stress of stillness   no motion in air?

Wings fall to earth
dark half-moons molting
to the bottom
they will go.

Dreaming gone.
Hanging down in rain gone.
Wings spanning the sky
gone   even screeching gone.

The bird watches his world
on Utopia Parkway.
Always living. Always dying.
Never known. Never gone.

Grand Hotel Bon Port
(Grand Hotel Bon Port, Circa 1959–1960)

Jan Zlotnik Schmidt

The bird's white plumed
wings arch towards the heavens.

He looks not to an oblivion
offered by blue dark tides.

Not to a white-washed void framing his world.

Perhaps for the last time he gazes
at a bon port a stopping place

a refuge for abandoned souls.
A final hold on the real.

A blue harbor of light.

The Last Cockatoo Box
(Untitled Except for L'Abeille, Circa 1959–1960)

Jan Zlotnik Schmidt

His thin second finger scratches his cheek.
What next? He murmurs *The last*
box the bird's lemon yellow and white wings
gone   arched flight gone.

Minutes tick away like thick flakes
of snow falling almost imperceptibly.
He cuts out the form like a swan's elongated
white body a flat silhouette a whelk of being.

He places the white cutout upright in the box.
A blue tracing like a second self. Outlines its feathers.
The torso takes up space the way words
or magic once could transform a world.

Next he presses the point of the pen
down to paper. One black eye emerges
staring into shadowed space.
He adds a white barbed wire
fencing the bird in. A barred universe.

What else to add? He ponders.
A scrap of newsprint *L'abeille.*
Ideas start buzzing in his head.
A garden. Bees foxglove primrose honey.
Sparks of light. What lurks in dreams.

We are all stripped bare he thinks.
Memories fade past selves disappear.
He craves remembered presence.
A brightness that can't be named.

Part IV

A World Apart

Joseph Cornell's Bubble Box and "The Man Blowing Bubbles"

Jan Zlotnik Schmidt

(About Jean Simeon Chardin's "Soap Bubbles")

Once upon a time an artist, tall and lanky, with haunted eyes, stares at a painting. A man, wearing a brown serge suit, blows a large soap bubble through a long thin white straw. The bubble is larger than the face of the little boy, gazing upwards at it. Looking in awe. The scene is shaded in brown, the bubble slightly iridescent. The artist sees the wonder in the boy's eyes—the way the boy is amazed by the sheer magic of the bubble. That glistening globe.

Later this man remembers the painting. Remembers the boy's glee at the sight of the soap bubble, suspended in air. He stares at an empty wooden frame, an empty wooden box. Then his imagination takes over. At the bottom of the box, a clay pipe with an ivory bowl, homage to his Dutch ancestors. Against the white background, he places cut-outs of shells encased in soap bubbles: a whorled white whelk, a fluted scallop shard. A large flat clam or abalone shell, a blackened mass like a miniature storm cloud in its center, then a larger one, like a womb, a fetus curled inside. In another, the close-up of an eye, the white dusted in grey-black, hints of an iris and pupil. Other shells shaped like ash leaves drift as if caught in a breeze.

All dizzying bursts of memory. Does he see a lonely man walking on a beach, scavenging for treasure? Or an innocent child whose life was once filled with wonder? The flick of his father's fingers in a card trick or the dazzle of candies and charms falling out of his father's suit pockets. Penny arcades, vaudeville and Wild West shows, and Luna Park at Coney Island. The merry go round of life with his family before death brought its own form of darkness.

Times encased in bubbles of memory ready to burst but still hovering in consciousness.

My Box Smells Like Old Cigarettes

Tana Miller

when Joseph Cornell's father died his childhood
burst into dust like an October puffball
years later he tried to replace whatever he could
scouring junk stores dimes stores gutters   gathered small

dolls balls blocks spinning tops   took them home
arranged rearranged them in boxes   forever
static   safe under glass   a lullaby   a poem
a permanent ode to childhood's treasure

I (not likely) to create my own childhood's shrine
might gather the shards that rained everywhere
the night mama threw her Haviland china in a straight line
at daddy's slobbery-drunk head   add stinking stale air

from one of their stuffed-to-the-top ashtrays
& put my childhood memories on display

The Medici Slot Machine

Tana Miller

Marchese Massimiliano Stampa
was no ordinary rascal twitchy boy

dark suit   ruffled collar
he stands forever still in his portrait
painted by Artemisia Gentileschi
stares with dark saucer
eyes at something   or is it someone?

he is frozen   motherless   morose
did Joseph Cornell see his half-orphan
self when he studied the Medici
princeling's portrait?

did he use this image
over and over like Warhol's soup cans
because he was also an orphan
whose life tumbled into fly-by-night
when his debt-ridden father died
and his mother had to raise
four children without laughter or money?

did Cornell attempt forever more
to rein in life?   to box it?
to glass over it?
to reduce life to myriad rectangles
maps   cut-outs   bubbles
jacks   dolls   blocks   balls
gather a safe world?

The Blue Peninsula

Jan Zlotnik Schmidt

(Inspired by Emily Dickinson's poem, "It might be lonelier," Poem #405)

He wonders about that blue white space in his heart.
Or a place where a touch of fingertips combats the cold
of a glance. Or the purple of his lips turning to a hyacinth blue
wash of a bare barbed wired window pane. He sees a faint blue
hush of sky. Circling miniature planets and puffs of clouds.

He presses his hands together as if in prayer.
He lives on his own blue peninsula of desire, regret, longing.

Bebe Marie

Tana Miller

Joseph Cornell visited his cousin Ethel
begged her to give him her childhood doll
Joseph insisted he had to protect Bebe Marie
poor Ethel   never a match for Joseph's passion
placed her doll in her cousin's arms
bid them both good bye

on the bus ride home Cornell
sniffed Bebe Marie's hair   her dress
inspected her yellowed petticoat
straightened her flower bedecked hat
touched the tip of his tongue
against her cold alabaster cheek
stared into her sightless eyes

did Cornell suspect she was
the child of the sun and the moon?
did he imagine the eons upon eons
she faithfully drove her parents' carriage
across the arc of the sky chased by howling
red-eyed Viking wolves hell-bent
on swallowing her mother   her father   the stars
bringing on the end-times   the forever darkness? *

at home Cornell sat at the kitchen table
selected a box   papered painted it
clipped twigs flowers from his backyard
hid her behind them glassed her in   whispered:
you are safe now my sweet
rest rest   when the time is right
you will dance across the velvet dark
forever holding hands with the stars

*Norse saga about the sun/moon's child taken from Snorri Sturluson's *Prose Edda*

Through a Glass, Darkly

Jan Zlotnik Schmidt

How did his own eyes peer
into his glass-bound world?
Were they piercing dots of light
sparks of fallen stars? The last trace
of Venus in a night sky?

How did they see whirls of constellations?
The rings of Saturn? Sagittarius
Orion and his Belt? Star maps?
Contained cosmos?

How did his gaze take in the swish
of Hedy Lamar's dark hair? The tulle
and feathers of a Swan Lake prima ballerina?
Shivers coursing through him,
his pursed lips staining the glass.

How did he press his nose to the pane
penetrate worlds   gaze at folds and fragments
of newsprint flown birds now staged on twigs
as if humming time could tumble away?

Through the glass darkly
he saw his own imaginative swagger
his wavering reflection shadowed
against the ruins of time.

Cornell and the Sparrows

Jan Zlotnik Schmidt

The boy peers through the half-open window,
presses his fingers against the peeling wood frame,
and steps into a dust filtered stream of light.

Inside, the man, pale, arms thin
as bamboo stalks, stretches his arms wide,
a resting place for sparrows.

They perch on the man's shoulders, head, arms,
scratch at his flesh peck at seeds spread
like confetti on the Formica kitchen table.

He wonders why the man let these birds into his house.

Sometimes the man is in the garden. He gives him things,
a silver ring, a cork ball, a flattened cut-out of a mermaid,
a rabbit's foot, as grey as dust, fur matted down.

Keep it for good luck, he said.
Once the man gave him pencil and paper
taught him to sketch a swan, a cloud, a star.

The man sits still in dimming light.

He listens to the singing birds. The boy doesn't know
he lives in a boxed in world of constellations,
emptied planets, circling moons.

Dreaming his ancient bones to sleep.

Biography of Joseph Cornell

Joseph Cornell was born in Nyack, New York, on Christmas Eve in 1903, the first child born to Joseph Cornell Sr., who worked as a textile designer, and Helen Ten Broeck Storms Cornell. Both parents were from socially prominent, Old Dutch ancestry. Joseph was followed by the births of two sisters, Helen and Elizabeth, and by his brother, Robert, who suffered from cerebral palsy.

He and his family lived in a large home in Nyack. His parents were active and entertained often, and the children enjoyed vacations and holidays with friends and relatives and special family trips into New York City. However, when his father died of leukemia in 1917, the halcyon life the family had lived ended. Joseph's mother was left penniless and indebted.

With financial assistance from her deceased husband's employer, Joseph was sent to Phillips Academy, where he did not thrive. He left without graduating and returned home to help his mother, who had moved the family to less expensive housing and held several part-time jobs to support them. His sisters soon married and moved away, and Joseph, Robert, and their mother settled on Utopia Highway in Queens, New York.

Joseph obtained employment as a textile salesperson and, an ardent self-learner, soon became interested in opera, theater, and visual art, although film remained his main interest. He became fascinated with many topics, from ballet to movie stars, to birds, to anything French, to the cosmos. A collector, he scoured dime stores, junk shops, used book stores, accumulating bits and pieces, taking it all home. He also began to purchase original art, drawings and shadow boxes, especially after wandering into the Julien Levy Gallery, where he became a regular visitor, and seeing vanguard European art, especially Surrealistic works.

As his interest in visual art grew, Joseph began experimenting with creating collages and assemblages housed in glass-fronted boxes. Slowly, he began to make many artist friends, visit art galleries and museums regularly and sell and show his own work. He was self-taught and never fit neatly into any category or school of art. He also continued his life-long passion for film, making several short films himself. He managed to produce a large body of artwork despite being forced to hold a variety of full and part-time jobs. He did most of his personal artwork late at night and on weekends. He never travelled, but he made many friends through his art and his Christian Science faith. Joseph never married, but he remained close to his family throughout his life, living with his mother and his disabled brother until they both died and visiting his sisters often. He frequented his favorite diners, coffee shops and dime stores in New York City and invited artist friends to visit him on Utopia Parkway for tea and sweets.

Children were special to Joseph, as was childhood itself. His last exhibit was for children, arranged with great personal care and displayed at a child-friendly height at a gallery at the Cooper Union in New York City in 1972. At the opening, cherry soda and brownies were served to the many school children invited, and Joseph Cornell was there in person to answer the children's questions.

Joseph Cornell died on December 29, 1972. Today, this brilliant, self-taught, loving, eccentric artist's work is highly regarded and displayed in major museums all over the world.

About Tana Miller

Tana Miller, during a thirty-year teaching career, has authored language arts curriculum guides for her school district, co-founded and facilitated a grade 5–8 annual literary magazine, presented whole language workshops in Hudson Valley schools and at the New York State Reading Conference. Tana co-founded and participated as a volunteer for ten years at a book group at Danbury Federal Prison for Women in Danbury, Connecticut. Since her retirement she has been an active volunteer at several food pantries and soup kitchens as well as an activist for the cause of racial justice. Her poetry has been published in several feminist journals and in *Writing in A Woman's Voice, Slant of Light* (Codhill Press), *An Apple in Her Hand* (co-author, Codhill Press), and *Rethinking the Ground Rules* (co-author, Mediacs Books). She has taught creative writing as well as memoir writing at Lifespring Institute, Saugerties, New York.

Tana cannot remember one day in her life when she didn't spend some time reading. She also considers her flock of eleven grandchildren as the most interesting people she knows.

About Jan Zlotnik Schmidt

Jan Zlotnik Schmidt is a SUNY Distinguished Teaching Professor Emerita at SUNY New Paltz in the Department of English where she taught autobiography, creative writing, American and contemporary literature, Women's Literature, and Holocaust Literature courses. Her work has been published in many journals including *Alaska Quarterly Review, Broadkill Review, Cream City Review, Home Planet News, Kansas Quarterly, Memoir (and), Vassar Review,* and *Westchester Review.* Her work has also been nominated for the Pushcart Prize Series. She has had two volumes of poetry published by the Edwin Mellen Press (*We Speak in Tongues,* 1991; *She had this memory,* 2000) and two collections of autobiographical essays, *Women/Writing/ Teaching* (SUNY Press, 1998) and *Wise Women: Reflections of Teachers at Mid-Life,* co-authored with Dr. Phyllis R. Freeman (Routledge, 2000). In addition, she co-authored with Laurence Carr an anthology of women's writing from the Hudson Valley: *A Slant of Light: Contemporary Women Writers of the Hudson Valley* (Codhill, 2013), which won the USA Best Book Award for an anthology. One chapbook, *The Earth Was Still,* was published by Finishing Line Press and another, *Hieroglyphs of Father-Daughter Time,* was published by Word Temple Press. Her full-length volume, *Foraging for Light,* was published in 2019 by Finishing Line Press. Recently a chapbook about the life of Bess Houdini, *Over the Moon Gone: The Vanishing Act of Bess Houdini,* was published by Palooka Press. Her poetry has been anthologized in *An Apple in Her Hand* (co-author, Codhill Press), *Rethinking the Ground Rules* (co-author, Mediacs Books). She has taught creative writing as well as memoir writing at Lifespring Institute, Saugerties, New York. She has been a frequent reader of her poetry at venues in the Hudson Valley.

www.ingramcontent.com/pod-product-compliance
Lightning Source LLC
Chambersburg PA
CBHW030916170426
43193CB00009BA/870